MANCHESTER
UNITED
THE OFFICIAL ANNUAL 2015

Written by Steve Bartram and Gemma Thompson
Designed by Chris Dalrymple
Cover design by Daniel James

© 2014. Published by Grange Communications Ltd., Edinburgh, under licence from Manchester United Football Club. Printed in the EU.

ISBN: 978-1-908925-69-5

£7.99

CONTENTS

INTRODUCTION

Hello and welcome to the 2015 Manchester United Annual.

These are exciting times at Old Trafford and the Aon Training Complex. After the disappointment of the 2013/14 season, everyone is focused on ensuring the 2014/15 campaign is one to remember.

Louis van Gaal's installation provided the Reds with a highly-decorated manager with a track record and character perfectly suited to one of the biggest jobs in football. We profile the vastly experienced Dutchman and his coaching team within these pages, as well as reliving the epic career of his assistant manager, Ryan Giggs.

The Reds' bid to return to splendour hinges on the work of the backroom staff and their squad, including the summer's new recruits. The 2015 Annual looks in detail at all the playing staff – with a special focus on captain Wayne Rooney's decade at the club – plus a sneak peek behind the scenes at what happens on the club's training pitches.

Once you've delved deeper into the world of United, it's time to test your knowledge of the Reds with a series of quizzes and puzzles, and you can also enter an exclusive competition to win a signed home 2014/15 shirt.

Enjoy!

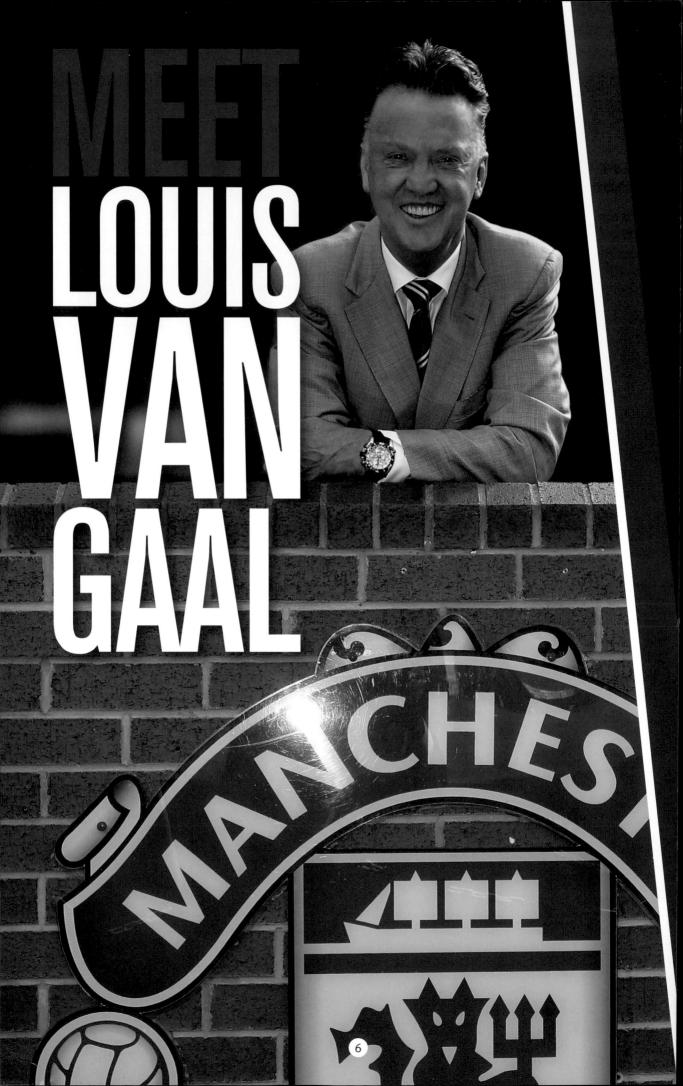

MEET
LOUIS
VAN
GAAL

Last May's appointment of Louis van Gaal as United boss represented a major coup for the Reds, with the capture of a manager steeped in success at the highest level.

A UEFA Champions League and UEFA Cup winner, plus a league champion in three different countries, the well-travelled Dutchman arrived at Old Trafford at the end of his second spell in charge of the Netherlands national team.

Renowned as a master motivator and committed to attacking football, van Gaal came to Manchester with a reputation seemingly built for United. Everyone is very excited about this new phase in the club's history," said executive vice chairman Ed Woodward. "His track record of success in winning leagues and cups across Europe throughout his career makes him the perfect choice for us."

Success with a swagger has been van Gaal's way since he broke into coaching and management after a 15-year playing career as a midfielder with Ajax, Royal Antwerp, Telstar, Sparta Rotterdam and AZ Alkmaar. After spells as assistant manager with AZ and Ajax he replaced Leo Beenhakker as the Amsterdam giants' manager in 1991, and before long had flooded the team with exceptional homegrown talents.

Under van Gaal, Ajax won three successive Dutch league titles, the UEFA Champions League and UEFA Cup, a run of success which alerted Barcelona to the manager's abilities. Glory followed van Gaal to Spain, with Barca immediately ending a three year wait for the La Liga title and then retaining the title, but his third term in Catalonia yielded only a second-placed finish and he left to manage the Dutch national team.

TROPHY CABINET

Van Gaal won silverware aplenty before he joined United...

Bayern Munich
Bundesliga: 2009/10
DFB-Pokal: 2009/10
DFB-Supercup: 2010

AZ Alkmaar
Eredivisie: 2008/09

Barcelona
La Liga: 1997/98, 1998/99
Copa del Rey: 1997/98
UEFA Super Cup: 1997

Ajax
UEFA Champions League: 1994/95

UEFA Cup: 1991/92

UEFA Super Cup: 1995

Intercontinental Cup: 1995

Eredivisie: 1993/94, 1994/95, 1995/96

KNVB Cup: 1992/93

Johan Cruyff Shield: 1993, 1994, 1995

Other
World Soccer Manager of the Year: 1995
Dutch Sports Coach of the Year: 2009
German Football Manager of the Year: 2010

The Catalans invited van Gaal back for a short-lived second stint just two years later, but it was back in Holland where success waited. AZ Alkmaar had only ruled the Dutch league once in their history but, in their fourth season under van Gaal, blew away all opposition and clinched the prize by a staggering 11-point margin.

Once again, success provoked attention, and Bayern Munich soon came calling. For the second time, van Gaal immediately won the league title in his first season in charge in a foreign country, becoming the first Dutch manager to win the Bundesliga. Bayern also won the domestic cup and went into the Champions League final chasing the Treble, having eliminated United on away goals in the quarter-finals. Instead it was José Mourinho's Internazionale who reigned in Madrid, and a year later van Gaal began his second stint as Netherlands manager.

He led his country to the 2014 World Cup in Brazil, where reigning champions Spain were obliterated in the Dutch's opening game, a result which heightened expectations of van Gaal's looming move to Old Trafford – a deal agreed shortly before the tournament. "It was always a wish for me to work in the Premier League," admitted the Dutchman. "To work as a manager for Manchester United, the biggest club in the world, makes me very proud. This club has big ambitions; I too have big ambitions. Together I'm sure we will make history."

Following the disappointment of the 2013/14 campaign, the installation of a manager with such an outstanding track record with some of European football's biggest clubs, hopes are high that van Gaal and United will prove to be an outstanding match for one another.

9

THE MEN BEHIND THE MANAGER

Louis van Gaal's appointment as United manager also prompted the introduction of a few new faces – and an extremely familiar one – to Old Trafford's home dugout. Meet the Reds' new backroom staff...

RYAN GIGGS, ASSISTANT MANAGER

Not a new appointment as such, but a promotion for United's record appearance-maker after he finally ended his epic playing career in May 2014. A player-coach last year but now assistant manager, the Welshman is already gearing up to be a key component of van Gaal's think tank at the Aon Training Complex. "I'm very pleased with Ryan," said the Dutchman. "My first impression of him was already good, and it keeps improving. You have to work very hard when you're my assistant – it's not always a pleasant job! But he's doing well, very well and I'm very happy he's on my staff."

ALBERT STUIVENBERG, ASSISTANT COACH

"This is a unique opportunity that has come my way," said Albert Stuivenberg, after being appointed United's assistant coach after just a year of working with van Gaal in the Dutch national setup. The former Netherlands under-21s coach, who also enjoyed success with the country's under-17s, has certainly made a lasting impression on his boss. "He has so much talent, this boy," said van Gaal. "I picked him up in the Dutch federation, he did a remarkable job and that's why I want to reward him to be my assistant here as a coach."

FRANS HOEK, GOALKEEPER COACH

A vastly experienced goalkeeper coach who has worked at Ajax, Barcelona and Bayern Munich, as well as with the Poland national team, Frans Hoek is renowned within football as one of the best in his field. Hoek has enjoyed a fine working relationship with van Gaal for over two decades, and he is cited by legendary Reds goalkeeper Edwin van der Sar as a major influence. "He groomed me and helped me learn all the things I needed to know to be a successful footballer over a lot of years," said the Champions League-winning goalkeeper.

MAX RECKERS, PERFORMANCE ANALYST

The advent of sports science and statistical analysis was embraced by United before most other major clubs, and Max Reckers became a key addition to an already impressive setup on van Gaal's insistence. The United manager admitted: "He's not only my computer guru - he's also nearly my son! Max collects all the data that we need, and we have a lot of data because in Manchester United, already there was a philosophy that you have to measure everything. It's unbelievable, what kind of data they have and what organisation you have to make for such a big club."

MARCEL BOUT, OPPOSITION SCOUT

A specialist in developing young talent and scouting opponents, Marcel Bout first crossed paths with van Gaal in 2006 when the pair worked together at AZ Alkmaar. The Dutch minnows soon shocked Holland by winning the Eridivisie title, and Bout was recruited by van Gaal when the latter moved to Bayern Munich. Again, success followed the pairing, and although they parted company when van Gaal left Bayern, they were soon working closely again in the Dutch national setup, with Bout a key member of the nation's under-21 backroom team. His role with United is to scout forthcoming opponents.

AIMING FOR PERFECTION

The Aon Training Complex is the setting for the players' day-to-day training work which is planned, managed and deployed by Louis van Gaal and his dedicated staff...

The eyes of the world are upon the United team every time the Reds step out for a game at home and abroad, but very few are privy to the inner workings of the team's match preparations at the Aon Training Complex. The club's state-of-the-art training ground is where Louis van Gaal, his coaching staff and players spend hours working on squad fitness, recovery and recuperation and tactics before and after each game, with the manager himself heavily involved in every training session. And everyone at United hopes that all the practice on the training pitch leads to perfection, or as close to it as possible, on matchday...

"Every day in training we all have to go out and show the manager what we can do and show the different qualities we have as players and a team. Everyone wants to impress a new manager with different ideas - we have to train well and listen to what he wants us to do and take that onto the pitch on matchday."
-Wayne Rooney

"Working with [goalkeeping coach] Frans [Hoek] is great and we learn from him every day. He wants quality – that's the big thing he's talked to us about. The manager and his coaches laid down the new rules pretty quickly when we all got together at the start of pre-season so everyone knows what is expected of them."

-Sam Johnstone

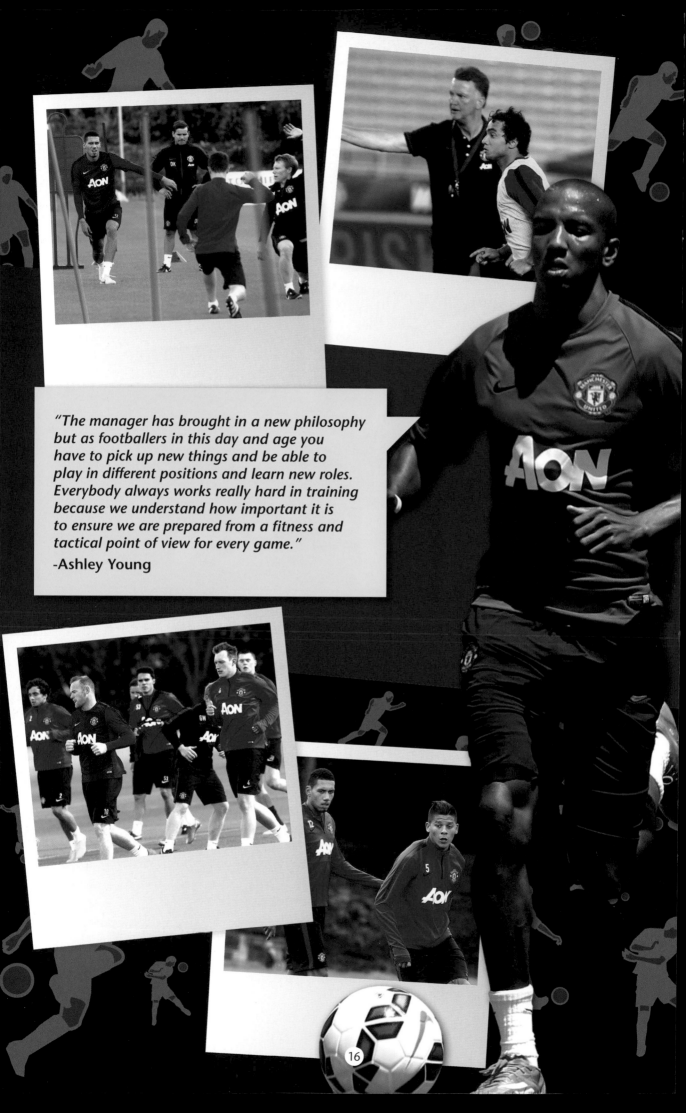

"The manager has brought in a new philosophy but as footballers in this day and age you have to pick up new things and be able to play in different positions and learn new roles. Everybody always works really hard in training because we understand how important it is to ensure we are prepared from a fitness and tactical point of view for every game."

-Ashley Young

"The manager is a great character. He is a leader who demands respect and discipline and his planning is meticulous, right down to meeting for breakfast, and for lunch, and even the team meetings that we have, plus the training has been fantastic. Everything is structured and really detailed. I think the lads have enjoyed all the things that he has introduced which are a little bit different."

-Ryan Giggs

PLAYER PROFILES

GOALKEEPERS

1. DAVID DE GEA
13. ANDERS LINDEGAARD
40. BEN AMOS
50. SAM JOHNSTONE

DEFENDERS

2. RAFAEL
3. LUKE SHAW
4. PHIL JONES
5. MARCOS ROJO
6. JONNY EVANS

12. CHRIS SMALLING
38. MIKE KEANE
41. REECE JAMES
42. TYLER BLACKETT

MIDFIELDERS

7. ANGEL DI MARIA
8. JUAN MATA
11. ADNAN JANUZAJ
16. MICHAEL CARRICK
17. DALEY BLIND
18. ASHLEY YOUNG

21. ANDER HERRERA
24. DARREN FLETCHER
25. ANTONIO VALENCIA
28. ANDERSON
31. MAROUANE FELLAINI
35. JESSE LINGARD

FORWARDS

9. RADAMEL FALCAO
10. WAYNE ROONEY
20. ROBIN VAN PERSIE
48. WILL KEANE
49. JAMES WILSON

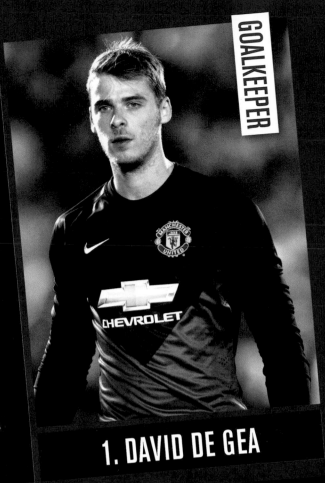

Born: 7 November 1990; Madrid, Spain

Previous clubs: Atletico Madrid

Joined United: 1 July 2011

United debut: 7 August 2011 vs Manchester City (N), Community Shield

International team: Spain

Signed from Atletico Madrid with a huge reputation and the enormous task of replacing the retired Edwin van der Sar, David rode out a rocky start to life at United to soon validate the faith placed in him by Sir Alex Ferguson and his staff. Showcasing his phenomenal athleticism, reflexes and temperament with mature consistency, the young Spaniard has established himself as one of world football's best stoppers.

Memorable moment: The undoubted star of United's troubled 2013/14 season, De Gea moved legendary goalkeeper Peter Schmeichel to hail "one of the best saves ever in the Premier League", after a stunning stop from Sunderland's Emanuele Giaccherini in October 2013.

1. DAVID DE GEA

Born: 13 April 1984; Dyrup, Denmark

Previous clubs: Odense Boldklub, Kolding FC (loan), Aalesunds FK

Joined United: 4 January 2011

United debut: 29 January 2011 vs Southampton (A), FA Cup

International team: Denmark

While the outstanding form of David De Gea may have limited Lindegaard's first team outings, the Dane has shown his quality whenever called upon. Signed during the 2010/11 campaign, his composure, good feet and excellent reflexes have proved him to be an excellent deputy. He played an important role in the Reds' 20th league title triumph and was in goal for Sir Alex Ferguson's final match in charge as manager.

Memorable moment: A keen United fan, Anders realised a boyhood dream when he collected his first-ever Premier League winners' medal in 2013, having made 13 appearances.

13. ANDERS LINDEGAARD

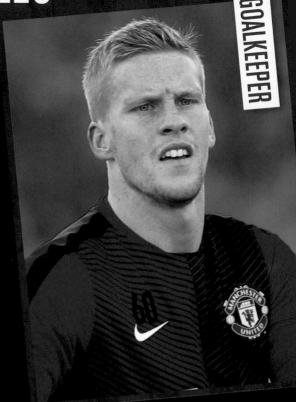

GOALKEEPER

Born: 10 April 1990; Macclesfield

Previous clubs: Trainee, Peterborough United (loan), Molde (loan), Oldham Athletic (loan), Hull City (loan), Carlisle United (loan)

Joined United: 1 July 2006

United debut: 23 September 2008 vs Middlesbrough (H), Carling Cup

International team: England (youth)

Patience has been a virtue in the United career of Academy product Ben Amos. The hulking 24-year-old was just 18 when he made his Reds bow, but was restricted to making just six more appearances in as many years as he vied with rivals replete with greater first team experience. The former England youth international has instead learned his trade throughout a variety of loan spells and has taken different lessons from each.

Memorable moment: Having rested David De Gea, Sir Alex Ferguson handed Amos his Premier League debut against Stoke in 2012, and Ben repaid his manager's faith with a faultless display and a clean sheet.

40. BEN AMOS

GOALKEEPER

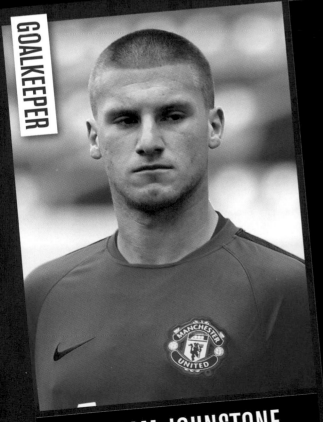

Born: 25 March 1993; Preston

Previous clubs: Trainee, Oldham Athletic (loan), Scunthorpe United (loan), Walsall (loan), Yeovil Town (loan), Doncaster Rovers (loan)

Joined United: 1 July 2009

United debut: N/A

International team: England (youth)

Sam is highly thought of at Old Trafford and has also made a steady progression through the England ranks at youth international level. Part of the club's FA Youth Cup-winning side in 2011, the agile stopper has also garnered vital experience from his handful of loan spells with sides across the lower divisions. He committed his future to the club in early 2014 by signing a new deal until June 2017.

Memorable moment: Johnstone was United's man between the posts as the Reds sealed a record-extending 10th FA Youth Cup triumph in May 2011, thanks to a 6-3 aggregate victory over Sheffield United.

50. SAM JOHNSTONE

Born: 9 July 1990; Rio de Janeiro, Brazil

Previous club: Fluminense

Joined United: 1 July 2008

United debut: 17 August 2008 vs Newcastle (H), Premier League

International team: Brazil

A favourite among supporters, the hundred-miles-an-hour Brazilian full-back carries an infectious joy in his approach to the game. Having arrived at the club in 2008 with his twin brother Fabio, who left the Reds in 2013, Rafael gradually made the right-back slot his own ahead of an injury-hit 2013/14 season. His breathless commitment to both defending and attacking demonstrate his total devotion to the cause.

Memorable moment: The Brazilian's outstanding campaign with United came in 2012/13, and contained an early flash of brilliance with a sublime, left-footed equaliser in the Reds' 2-1 win over Liverpool at Anfield.

DEFENDER

2. RAFAEL

DEFENDER

4. PHIL JONES

Born: 21 February 1992; Preston

Previous club: Blackburn Rovers

Joined United: 1 July 2011

United debut: 7 August 2011 vs Manchester City (N), Community Shield

International team: England

Having impressed in a handful of performances against the Reds for Blackburn Rovers, the powerful, energetic defender chose Old Trafford over several alternative destinations in the summer of 2011. Though he has performed admirably in central midfield when required to, the bullish England international has proven himself to be an outstanding defender when he has managed to avoid the injury woes which have punctuated his Reds career to date.

Memorable moment: Though he sees himself as a centre-back, Jones' impressive versatility was underlined against Arsenal in November 2013, when he spent half the game in midfield and half in defence, excelling in both.

DEFENDER

Born: 3 January 1988; Belfast, Northern Ireland

Previous clubs: Trainee, Royal Antwerp (loan), Sunderland (loan)

Joined United: 1 July 2004

United debut: 26 September 2007 vs Coventry City (H), League Cup

International team: Northern Ireland

A product of United's renowned youth system, Jonny has grown into one of the most accomplished, intelligent and unflappable centre-backs around. Injuries have hampered his progress at times, but he remains an excellent reader of the game, calm on the ball and brave having learnt from two of the best in Rio Ferdinand and Nemanja Vidic. After taking almost five years to net his first goal in 2012, he's since chipped in with some key strikes.

Memorable moment: Jonny was part of the United defence which helped Edwin van der Sar break the Premier League clean sheet record in 2008/09 on the way to title glory.

6. JONNY EVANS

DEFENDER

Born: 22 November 1989; Greenwich

Previous clubs: Maidstone United, Fulham

Joined United: 7 July 2010

United debut: 8 August 2010 vs Chelsea (N), Community Shield

International team: England

Having risen from non-league Maidstone United to the Reds within just three years, Chris Smalling's career so far has been a remarkable one – even if he has been dogged by injury. Now a full England international, the former Fulham starlet has been utilised as a makeshift right-back on occasion, but retains his preference to permanently nail down a central defensive berth at Old Trafford.

Memorable moment: An imposing target man in the opposition box, Smalling's most important goal to date was a powerful early header to set the Reds en route to victory over perennial title rivals Chelsea in September 2011.

12. CHRIS SMALLING

Born: 11 January 1993; Stockport

Previous clubs: Trainee, Leicester City (loan), Derby County (loan), Burnley (loan)

Joined United: 1 July 2009

United debut: 25 October 2011 vs Aldershot Town (A), League Cup

International team: England (youth)

One of the brightest young defensive prospects in the English game, Mike Keane is a powerful presence who has developed startlingly in both physical and technical terms in recent seasons. Whether on the deck or in the air, in the centre of defence or at full-back, the Stockport-born youngster – who is the twin brother of Reds striker Will - looks certain to have a bright future.

Memorable moment: Though Chelsea ultimately won the tie in extra-time, Keane's display in a November 2012 League Cup defeat at Stamford Bridge displayed his brimming confidence and assuredness at the top level.

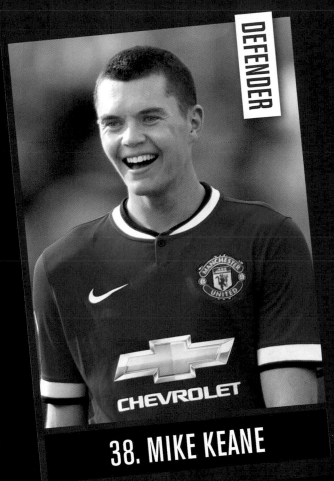

38. MIKE KEANE

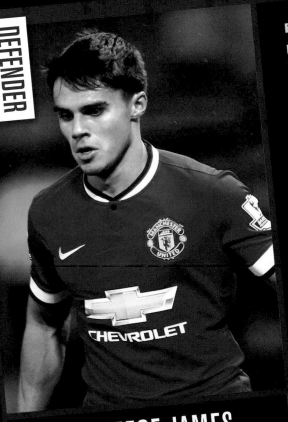

Born: 7 November 1993; Bacup

Previous clubs: Rossendale United, Blackburn Rovers, Preston North End, Carlisle United (loan)

Joined United: 1 July 2012

United debut: 26 August 2014 vs MK Dons (A), League Cup

International team: N/A

A regularly impressive figure for Warren Joyce's under-21s since his 2012 arrival, Reece was nevertheless one of the surprise packages of United's 2014 pre-season tour. By trade a left-back and occasionally a midfielder, the youngster - whose brother Matty was on United's books until his transfer to Leicester City - was used as Louis van Gaal's left wing-back and duly demonstrated his ability to adapt to senior surroundings with some accomplished displays.

Memorable moment: Having never scored during his time in the Reds' youth ranks, a brace against LA Galaxy provided an unforgettable first United run-out for Reece. "I was in a bit of shock," he admitted, "and when the second one went in, I couldn't believe it was actually happening!"

41. REECE JAMES

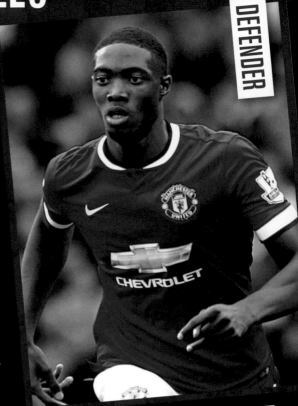

DEFENDER

Born: 2 April 1994; Manchester

Previous clubs: Blackpool (loan), Birmingham City (loan)

Joined United: 1 July 2002

United debut: 16 August 2014 vs Swansea City (H), Premier League

International team: England (youth)

A fixture in United's 2011 FA Youth Cup-winning side and an England international through various age groups, Tyler Blackett is a young defender of great pedigree. Armed with the experience of Championship loans with Blackpool and Birmingham City, the tall, powerful youngster took advantage of a chance to impress on United's pre-season tour of 2014, and he was handed his debut in the Reds' Premier League opener against Swansea for his efforts.

Memorable moment: Though defeat to the Swans took the edge off Tyler's afternoon, his individual display showcased his undoubted potential. There is still much for the young defender to learn, but his physicality, aerial prowess, calmness and passing gives him an impressive arsenal.

42. TYLER BLACKETT

MIDFIELDER

Born: 28 April 1988; Burgos, Spain

Previous clubs: Real Madrid, Valencia, Chelsea

Joined United: 25 January 2014

United debut: 28 January 2014 vs Cardiff City (H), Premier League

International team: Spain

A supremely gifted and intelligent footballer who can score and create goals, Juan signed for a club record fee at the time in the 2014 January transfer window from Chelsea. The Spanish World Cup and European Championship winner, who had caught the eye in English football's top flight during his highly successful reign at Stamford Bridge, impressed from the off at Old Trafford and has the ability to make an impact from either wing or just behind the striker.

Memorable moment: A week after opening his goals account against Aston Villa, the Spaniard laid on a Man of the Match performance and hit a brilliant brace in a 4-0 win at Newcastle, including an exquisite 20-yard free-kick.

8. JUAN MATA

Born: 5 February 1995; Brussels, Belgium

Previous club: Anderlecht

Joined United: 1 July 2011

United debut: 11 August 2013 vs Wigan Athletic (N), Community Shield

International team: Belgium

Talk about progress - just 10 months after making his United debut, Januzaj, who impressed throughout his time in the club's youth sides, was performing for Belgium at the World Cup in Brazil. His place in the Belgium side came on the back of a memorable first senior campaign for the Reds which included 35 appearances and four goals. Adnan has the ability to bamboozle defenders on either wing and possesses a real eye for goal.

Memorable moment: There's nothing like bagging a double on your Premier League debut to secure a comeback victory. That's exactly what Januzaj did in October 2013 when United beat Sunderland thanks to two superb strikes from the gifted Belgian.

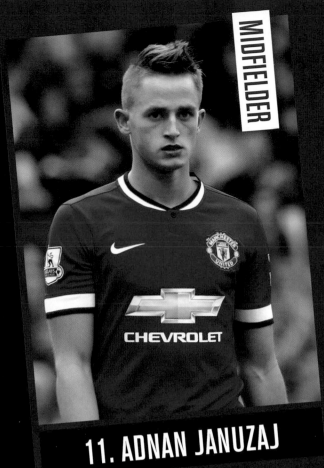

11. ADNAN JANUZAJ

Born: 29 July 1981; Wallsend

Previous clubs: West Ham United, Swindon (loan), Birmingham City (loan), Tottenham Hotspur

Joined United: 31 July 2006

United debut: 23 August 2006 vs Charlton Athletic (A), Premier League

International team: England

A deeper and deeper presence in the United midfield as his career has progressed, Michael Carrick has established himself as a purist's footballer who quietly damages opponents by breaking up attacks, holding possession and patiently picking the right pass. There is no such glory as that enjoyed by a regular goalscorer or an athletic goalkeeper, but Carrick's role as a midfield shield and deep-lying baton waver has been invaluable to United's modern successes.

Memorable moment: The duration of the 2012/13 season provided Carrick's career highlight, and the reward wasn't only his fifth title winners' medal; he was nominated for the PFA Player of the Year award.

16. MICHAEL CARRICK

PLAYER PROFILES

Born: 9 July 1985; Stevenage

Previous clubs: Watford, Aston Villa

Joined United: 1 July 2011

United debut: 7 August 2011 vs Manchester City (N), Community Shield

International team: England

Signed from Aston Villa in the summer of 2011, Ashley has the talent to make an impact from either flank or behind the main striker. As a quick and skilful winger or wing-back, Young gives United options on both sides and has also proved his worth in the goalscoring stakes from distance as well. He'll be determined to improve upon a couple of injury-ravaged and frustrating campaigns under his new manager in 2014/15.

Memorable moment: His sublime double in the stunning 8-2 victory over Arsenal at Old Trafford just a few weeks after his United bow. Young netted in either half with two unstoppable curling efforts.

18. ASHLEY YOUNG

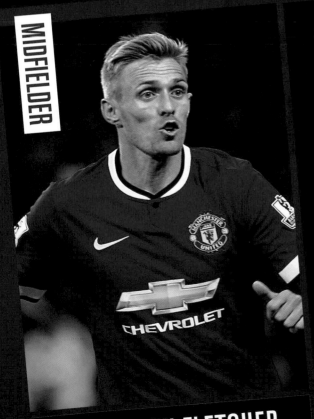

Born: 1 February 1984; Edinburgh, Scotland

Previous clubs: Trainee

Joined United: 3 July 2000

United debut: 12 March 2003 vs FC Basel (H), Champions League

International team: Scotland

The longest-serving player in Louis van Gaal's squad, the Scottish international midfielder, and now United's vice-captain, made his Reds debut as a teenager in 2003. Initially learning his trade alongside legendary skipper Roy Keane, the tenacious youngster developed into a key component of the Reds' approach, in particular against illustrious opposition. Though his career was disrupted for two years by a serious bowel condition, Fletcher displayed typical courage to overcome it and return to action.

Memorable moment: In November 2005, United were coming in for heavy criticism for lagging behind league leaders Chelsea but, when the Blues arrived at Old Trafford, it was Fletcher's looping header which sealed a famous victory.

24. DARREN FLETCHER

Born: 4 August 1985; Lago Agrio, Ecuador

Previous clubs: El Nacional, Villarreal, Recreativo (loan), Wigan Athletic

Joined United: 30 June 2009

United debut: 9 August 2009 vs Chelsea (N), Community Shield

International team: Ecuador

A powerful, pacey winger who can also turn his hand to full-back or wing-back duties, Ecuadorian international Antonio Valencia can be a defender's nightmare. An impressive first season at United in 2009/10 was followed by two serious injuries, but he recovered to sweep the board at United's 2011/12 end-of-season awards. A regular supplier and occasional scorer of goals, Antonio remains a potent weapon to have in the Reds' arsenal.

Memorable moment: Though the 2011/12 campaign ultimately ended in heartbreak, Valencia's thunderous late opener at Blackburn in a key late-season win prompted scenes of wild celebration both on and off the field.

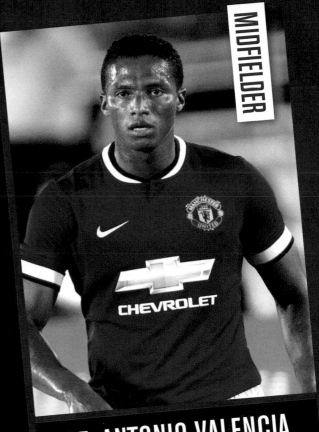

25. ANTONIO VALENCIA

28. ANDERSON

Born: 13 April 1988; Porto Alegre, Brazil

Previous clubs: Gremio, FC Porto, Fiorentina (loan)

Joined United: 1 July 2007

United debut: 1 September 2007 vs Sunderland (H), Premier League

International team: Brazil

Brazilian midfielder Anderson's career has been heavily disrupted by injuries during his time at Old Trafford. A highly-rated no.10 with Porto, his previous club, the talented middle man drifted back into a deeper role under the tutelage of Sir Alex Ferguson and caught the eye in a breath-taking first season in English football. In the ensuing years, however, his involvement has waned and he spent half of the 2013/14 term on loan at Fiorentina.

Memorable moment: An unknown quantity when he arrived in the Premier League, the no-nonsense Brazilian excelled against big-name opponents – none more than Steven Gerrard, who was overrun in the Reds' December 2007 win at Anfield.

MIDFIELDER

31. MAROUANE FELLAINI

Born: 22 November 1987; Etterbeek, Belgium

Previous clubs: Standard Liege, Everton

Joined United: 2 September 2013

United debut: 14 September 2013 vs Crystal Palace (H), Premier League

International team: Belgium

A persistent pest playing against United during his five years at Everton, Belgian international Marouane Fellaini arrived at Old Trafford as the first major signing of David Moyes' managerial reign at the club. A versatile midfielder who can also be deployed as a makeshift attacker, Fellaini will look to build on an unsettled first season at Old Trafford by displaying the form which prompted his big-money capture.

Memorable moment: Fellaini's Champions League debut for the Reds was a thrilling 4-2 victory over Bayer Leverkusen, in which the Belgian turned in an impressive display of destructive midfield play to disrupt the visitors' rhythm.

MIDFIELDER

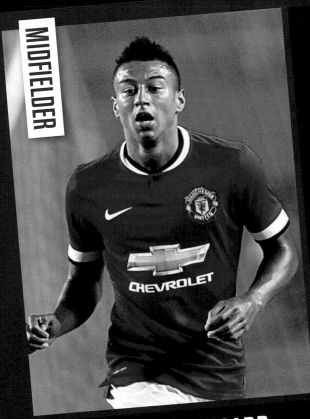

35. JESSE LINGARD

Born: 15 December 1992; Warrington

Previous clubs: Leicester City (loan), Birmingham City (loan), Brighton and Hove Albion (loan)

Joined United: 1 July 2009

United debut: 16 August 2014 vs Swansea City (H), Premier League

International team: England (youth)

A player who has excelled at both Reserve and Championship level during a couple of impressive loan periods, Jesse was handed his United debut by Louis van Gaal in the opening match of the 2014/15 campaign. It may have ended in disappointment for the attacker, who started at right wing-back, after injury forced him off early on, but Lingard has already shown he has the pace, skill and intelligence - as well as an eye for goal - to make an impact at the highest level if given the chance.

Memorable moment: Jesse was United's top scorer on the 2013 pre-season tour and he caught the eye again a year later when he came off the bench to confirm victory over arch rivals Liverpool the International Champions Cup final in Miami.

Born: 24 October 1985; Liverpool

Previous club: Everton

Joined United: 31 August 2004

United debut: 28 September 2004 vs Fenerbahce (H), Champions League

International team: England

United and England's talisman for the last few seasons, Wayne is as determined, influential and talented as they come. Named by Louis van Gaal as United's club captain, he is a player with the aptitude to score and create any kind of goal and gets equal satisfaction from doing both. Wazza, who is in United's all-time top three goalscorers, will do a job for the team anywhere on the pitch and is as good a poacher as he is a piledriver master from outside the area.

Memorable moment: It's hard to pick just one. A hat-trick on his United debut, that overhead kick against City and a goal from the half-way line at West Ham in 2014 are all perfect examples of why Rooney is top class.

10. WAYNE ROONEY

Born: 6 August 1983; Rotterdam, Netherlands

Previous clubs: Feyenoord, Arsenal

Joined United: 17 August 2012

United debut: 20 August 2012 vs Everton (A), Premier League

International team: Netherlands

Procured from Arsenal just months after United had been dethroned by Manchester City, Robin van Persie arrived at Old Trafford as one of world football's established stars. The Dutchman soon set about justifying the hype his 2012 arrival prompted, scoring a spate of vital goals, and by the end of the campaign, his slick, classy style had yielded 30 goals and the first league winners' medal of his career.

Memorable moment: After scoring the goals which took United to the brink of a 20th league title, Robin finished the job with a hat-trick against Aston Villa which included a sensational long-range volley.

20. ROBIN VAN PERSIE

PLAYER PROFILES

FORWARD

Born: 11 January 1993; Stockport

Previous clubs: Wigan Athletic (loan), Queens Park Rangers (loan)

Joined United: 1 July 2009

United debut: 31 December 2011 vs Blackburn Rovers (H), Premier League

International team: England (youth)

Rated by under-21s coach Warren Joyce as "probably the best player of his age in the country," at the time of his 2012 cruciate ligament injury, striker Will Keane has overcome adversity to return to the brink of first team football. Blessed with tremendous speed of thought and spatial awareness, the England youth striker scored an astonishing variety of goals during his climb through the United ranks, and his rare talent is ready to shine as and when he is given the platform.

Memorable moment: Though Will was only 18 when he made his senior debut against Blackburn Rovers, his finest accomplishment to date was joining the select band of names to win the club's Jimmy Murphy Young Player of the Year award in 2010.

48. WILL KEANE

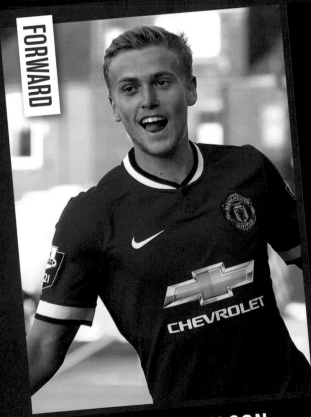

FORWARD

Born: 1 December 1995; Biddulph

Previous clubs: Trainee

Joined United: 1 July 2012

United debut: 6 May 2014 vs Hull City (H), Premier League

International team: England (youth)

The brief interim managerial reign of Ryan Giggs sprung an almighty shock in the Reds' final home game of 2013/14 against Hull City, with both James Wilson and Tom Lawrence handed surprise debuts. For keen observers of the Reds' youth ranks, the striker's speed of thought and penalty area prowess were well established, but the teenager caught the Tigers cold by bagging a close-range double in a 3-1 victory.

Memorable moment: Debuting for United at just 18 years of age is a rarity, but Wilson grasped his chance and became only the 13th player in the Reds' history to score more than once on his debut.

49. JAMES WILSON

NEW SIGNINGS

United smashed the British transfer record in the summer of 2014 with the capture of Angel Di Maria for £59.7million. His arrival came on the back of three other big-money signings - defenders Luke Shaw and Marcos Rojo and midfielder Ander Herrera. The Reds made their final move in the market on deadline day when Dutch international Daley Blind put pen to paper, and later that night the club pulled off the surprise coup of the summer when it was announced that Colombian striker Radamel Falcao would be joining. Here, we give you an insight into what United fans can expect to see from our summer additions, this season and beyond...

3. LUKE SHAW

Born: 12 July 1995; Kingston-upon-Thames
Position: Full-back
Previous clubs: Southampton
Joined United: 27 June 2014
International team: England

off an incredible few months by signing for the Reds.

A product of Southampton's successful youth system (Gareth Bale and Theo Walcott are fellow graduates), the left-back made his Saints debut as a 16-year-old in January 2012. Just a few months later Southampton were promoted back to English football's top flight and Shaw was handed a professional contract. He became a first-team regular thereafter which led to a senior England call-up, having progressed through the international youth ranks, and a nomination in the PFA Young Player of the Year category at the end of the 2013/14 season.

He made 67 appearances in all for the Saints before making the switch to Old Trafford at the end of June 2014. The full-back has also been trialled as a wing-back as van Gaal has experimented with different formational approaches, and there is no doubt the youngster's versatility will stand him in good stead for the lessons and challenges which lie ahead.

It's fair to say 2014 is a year that will live long in the memory of Luke Shaw. After winning his first England cap in March, helping Southampton to an impressive eighth-place finish in the Barclays Premier League and scooping a place in the PFA Team of the Year, Shaw became the youngest player to feature at the World Cup in Brazil and rounded

"I am thrilled and excited to have joined United. I want to continue to progress my career and this is the ideal place for me to do that. I am looking forward to this new chapter in my life and learning from the world-class players and management at the club."
Luke Shaw

5. MARCOS ROJO

Born: 20 March 1990; La Plata, Argentina
Position: Defender
Previous clubs: Estudiantes, Spartak Moscow, Sporting Lisbon
Joined United: 20 August 2014
International team: Argentina

Faustino Marcos Alberto Rojo had made no secret of his desire to join the Reds in the days leading up to his signing from Sporting Lisbon. And he got his wish on 20 August when he completed his £16million move to Old Trafford on a five-year contract, with Nani going the other way for a season-long loan as part of the agreement.

The Argentinian international defender began his career with hometown club Estudiantes de La Plata where he won the Copa Libertadores, the most prestigious club competition in South American football, in 2009 and the Torneo Apertura (one part of Argentina's top-flight division) in 2010.

A move to Spartak Moscow followed in December 2010, but Rojo, an aggressive, brave and tough-tackling performer, struggled to settle and switched to Sporting Lisbon in July 2012. By that point he'd already made his international debut for Argentina and has since gone on to win over 27 caps. He impressed at left-back – he also played for Sporting as part of a three-man central defence during the 2014 World Cup as Argentina finished runners-up to Germany and he netted his first goal for his country in Brazil with the winner in the final group game against Nigeria.

Rojo, which means 'red' in Spanish, joins an elite group of Argentinians to play for United (which now includes international team-mate Angel Di Maria), following in the footsteps of former Estudiantes team-mate Juan Sebastian Veron, Gabriel Heinze and Carlos Tevez.

> "It is such an honour to say that I now play for Manchester United. The Premier League is the most exciting league in the world and to have the chance to play in it for the world's biggest club is a dream for me."
> **Marcos Rojo**

7. ANGEL DI MARIA

Born: 14 February 1988; Rosario, Argentina
Position: Attacking midfielder
Previous clubs: Rosario Central, Benfica, Real Madrid
Joined United: 26 August 2014
International team: Argentina

United smashed the British transfer record in August 2014 after securing the services of Angel Fabian Di Maria Hernandez from Real Madrid. The attacking midfielder and the Reds' new no.7 put pen to paper on a £59.7million deal citing United as the "only club I would have left Madrid for."

Di Maria began his career with Rosario Central in his homeland before a move to Benfica where he won the Primeira Liga in 2010 during his final campaign in Portugal. But it was in Madrid where he really caught the football world's attention as he helped Real win La Liga in 2012 and the Copa del Rey in 2011 and 2014, as well as the club's 10th European Cup in 2014 and most recently the UEFA Super Cup. An incisive dribbler and passer, no-one supplied more assists than Di Maria during the 2013/14 Spanish league campaign.

Di Maria has impressed at international level too, winning the 2008 Olympic Games with Argentina and helping them finish as runners-up at the 2014 World Cup where he was named on the 10-man shortlist for FIFA's Golden Ball award for the tournament's best player.

The 2014 Champions League winner, who was also named Man of the Match in Real's European triumph over Atletico Madrid in May 2014, not only brings pace, talent and a superb left foot, he is, according to van Gaal, "a world-class midfielder but most importantly a team player."

> "There were a lot of clubs interested in me, but United is the only one that I would have left Real Madrid for. I am impressed by the vision and determination everyone has here to get this club back to the top - where it belongs."
> **Angel Di Maria**

9. RADAMEL FALCAO

Born: 10 February 1986; Santa Marta, Colombia
Position: Forward
Previous clubs: Lanceros Boyaca, River Plate, FC Porto, Atletico Madrid, AS Monaco
Joined United: 1 September 2014
International team: Colombia

Signed out of the blue on the final day of the 2014 summer transfer window, Radamel Falcao stunned football with his move to Old Trafford.

The Colombian international is one of world football's deadliest marksmen and was coveted by several top clubs, before eventually choosing to leave Monaco for Manchester on a one-year loan, at the end of which United have the option to purchase him.

After rising through the ranks at Lanceros Boyaca, Falcao left Colombia to join Argentinian giants River Plate. He duly began scoring goals with eye-catching regularity and, while he experienced highs and lows with River, he starred in their 2008 title triumph before being snapped up by FC Porto the following year. Falcao quickly set the Portuguese league and Champions League alight with his prolific goalscoring and in 2010/11 he inspired Porto's league and Europa League Double. His form prompted a reunion with former manager Diego Simeone after the Argentinian took charge at Atletico Madrid, and there was no let-up in Falcao's scoring exploits as he helped his new team emulate his previous club by winning the Europa League and he scored a hat-trick in Atletico's UEFA Super Cup win over Chelsea in 2012.

Another big money move soon beckoned, to Monaco, but Falcao spent only one injury-ravaged season in France before his shock capture gave United one of the game's finest finishers.

> *"I am delighted to be working with Louis van Gaal and to have the chance to contribute to the team's success during this very exciting period in the club's history."*
>
> **Radamel Falcao**

17. DALEY BLIND

Born: 9 March 1990; Amsterdam, Netherlands
Position: Midfielder / defender
Previous clubs: Groningen (loan), Ajax
Joined United: 1 September 2014
International team: Netherlands

Daley Blind completed his £14million move to United from Ajax on transfer deadline day. The Netherlands international, who is comfortable either in defence or midfield, was well known to Louis van Gaal after the pair worked together in the Dutch national team.

Blind followed in his father Danny's footsteps by making his name at Ajax after progressing through the club's famous youth ranks. Daley impressed at left-back as Ajax won the Dutch Eredivisie title in 2011, 2012 and 2013 and at the end of the 2012/13 campaign he was named the club's Player of the Year. During 2013/14, he played as a holding midfielder and was named Dutch Footballer of the Year as Ajax won a fourth consecutive league title.

His impressive performances at club level resulted in international recognition and he won his first cap in February 2013 in a friendly against Italy. Blind was named in van Gaal's 2014 World Cup squad and started the opening match against Spain – resulting in a famous 5-1 win for the Netherlands - at left wing-back. He scored his first goal for his country in the 3-0 victory over hosts Brazil in the third-place play-off.

After enhancing his reputation on international football's biggest stage, Daley was handed a "dream" move to United, where van Gaal saw huge demand for his compatriot's versatility and tactical awareness in the ongoing transitional work at Old Trafford.

> *"I am very excited to be here. I think it's a good move for me to make now as a chance like this may never come again."*
>
> **Daley Blind**

21. ANDER HERRERA

Born: 14 August 1989; Bilbao, Spain
Position: Midfielder
Previous clubs: Real Zaragoza, Athletic Club
Joined United: 26 June 2014
International team: Spain (youth)

Having been a transfer target for United a year earlier, the Reds got their man in June 2014 as Ander Herrera became the first signing of the Louis van Gaal era.

The central midfielder arrived from Athletic Club in Bilbao after United triggered the buy-out clause in his contract. He came to Old Trafford with a burgeoning reputation having established himself as one of Spain's most promising young stars following successful

spells with Real Zaragoza and hometown team Athletic Club. He even impressed against the Reds in the UEFA Europa League in March 2012 when Herrera and his Athletic Club team-mates knocked Sir Alex Ferguson's men out of the competition at the last 16 stage.

While a mooted move to Old Trafford in the summer of 2013 never materialised, the Spanish playmaker enjoyed another fine campaign in 2013/14, netting five goals in 33 appearances as Athletic Club finished fourth in La Liga.

It's not just at club level where Herrera has caught the eye; he has starred for Spain's youth sides and was part of the 2011 UEFA European Under-21 Championship-winning squad, which also included fellow Reds David De Gea and Juan Mata. All three United stars started the final against Switzerland, with Herrera netting the first goal in a 2-0 victory and he'll be hoping to enjoy many more celebrations with his compatriots and his other United team-mates in the coming years.

> "Signing for Manchester United is a dream come true. I have played at Old Trafford for Athletic Club and it was one of the highlights of my career so far. I have joined United to do all I can to help the team reach its objectives."
> **Ander Herrera**

RECORD BREAKERS

United's £59.7million signing of Angel Di Maria was the ninth time the club has set a new British transfer record fee. Here's the Reds' history of topping the spending charts...

Date	Player	Signed from	Fee
August 1962	Denis Law	Torino	£110,000
February 1978	Gordon McQueen	Leeds United	£495,000
October 1981	Bryan Robson	West Bromwich Albion	£1,500,000
July 1993	Roy Keane	Nottingham Forest	£3,750,000
January 1995	Andrew Cole	Newcastle United	£7,000,000*
June 2001	Ruud van Nistelrooy	PSV Eindhoven	£19,000,000
July 2001	Juan Sebastian Veron	Lazio	£28,100,000
July 2002	Rio Ferdinand	Leeds United	£29,100,000
August 2014	Angel Di Maria	Real Madrid	£59,700,000

*Cole deal was for £6million plus Keith Gillespie, who was valued at £1million.

RYAN GIGGS
MAN FOR ALL SEASONS

The figures say it all - 963 appearances, 168 goals and 34 major honours spread across the course of an astonishing 24-season career – it's fair to say Ryan Giggs didn't do too badly in that famous red shirt...

1990/91
Ryan made his senior United debut, replacing Denis Irwin in a defeat to Everton on 2 March 1991. Two months later he netted his first goal for the club, a winner on his first league start against Manchester City, albeit via a huge deflection.

1991/92
Giggs collected his first senior trophy - the European Super Cup, before setting up Brian McClair to net the winner in the League Cup final. He was voted PFA Young Player of the Year and captained the famed 'Class of '92' to FA Youth Cup final victory.

1992/93
The winger helped the Reds win the inaugural Premier League title which was a first championship crown for the club in 26 years. He was also named PFA Young Player of the Year once again.

1993/94
Ryan played a major role in helping United retain the league title and helped the team complete a domestic Double following the 4-0 FA Cup final victory over Chelsea. This was his highest-scoring season in a red shirt with 17 goals.

1994/95
A rare trophyless season for Alex Ferguson's men who were majorly hampered by the eight-month suspension of Eric Cantona. Giggs finished the season on the sidelines, injured.

1995/96
Despite the loss of three key senior players in the summer of '95, the Reds roared back to glory, inspired by Cantona and 'the kids' as Messrs Giggs, Beckham, Scholes, Butt and the Nevilles helped United claim another domestic double.

1996/97
While Champions League glory continued to elude the Reds, Ryan was part of another title-winning side as United finished top of the pile once more.

1997/98
The team finished empty-handed as Arsenal claimed league glory, but few will forget Ryan's brilliant solo goal in the enthralling 3-2 win over Juventus at Old Trafford.

1998/99
The greatest season in the club's history ended with the capture of an unprecedented Treble and featured the goal that Ryan will forever be remembered for in the FA Cup semi-final replay win over Arsenal.

1999/00
The league title was retained once more, this time by a record winning margin of 18 points over runners-up Arsenal. Giggs was presented with the Man of the Match prize in the 1-0 victory over Palmeiras of Brazil in the Intercontinental Cup final in Tokyo.

2000/01

The Reds sealed a hat-trick of championship crowns and Ryan came third in a fans' poll for the greatest-ever United player behind Eric Cantona and George Best.

2001/02

The season began with a testimonial match for Ryan, marking a decade of excellent service, but ended in disappointment and a trophyless campaign for the team.

2002/03

After making his 500th appearance and netting his 100th goal for the club, Ryan was part of another title-winning season.

2003/04

The Reds had to settle for just the FA Cup this term but it was extra special for Giggs as victory over Millwall came at the Millennium Stadium in his city of birth, Cardiff.

2004/05

A season to forget for everyone at the club as Sir Alex's men finished third behind Chelsea and Arsenal and cruelly lost out to the latter on penalties in the FA Cup final.

2005/06

While United failed to qualify for the Champions League knockout stages and lost out in the title race to Chelsea, Wigan were thrashed in the League Cup final and Ryan was inducted into English football's Hall of Fame.

2006/07

Ryan claimed a record ninth championship winners' medal and helped the Reds reach the Champions League semi-finals where AC Milan proved a hurdle too many.

2007/08

50 years on from the Munich air disaster, Sir Alex's side claimed Champions League glory on penalties against Chelsea in Moscow with Giggs becoming the Reds' record appearance-maker, overtaking Sir Bobby Charlton, having come off the bench to equal the milestone a few days earlier and score in United's title-clinching victory at Wigan.

2008/09

United were named World Champions and went on to win the League Cup and yet another title. Despite the disappointment of losing the Champions League final to Barcelona, Ryan was named the PFA Players' Player of Year at the grand old age of 35.

2009/10

After being voted BBC Sports Personality of the Year for 2009, Ryan played a pivotal role in helping the team win the League Cup. He also netted his 150th goal for the club.

2010/11

The Reds may have lost out in the Champions League final to Barcelona, but becoming the most successful club in league football with a record 19th title, to overtake Liverpool's long-standing record, more than made up for the disappointment.

2011/12

Despite a season of no trophies, Ryan marked his 900th appearance for the club with an injury-time winner at Norwich and he was named captain of Great Britain's football team at the London Olympics.

2012/13

In Sir Alex's final season as manager, Giggs, who played his 1,000th professional match against Real Madrid, won a 13th title medal and his goal at home against Everton ensured he had scored in 23 consecutive league campaigns. His strike against QPR soon after would prove to be his final ever goal.

2013/14

After being named player-coach at the start of the season, Giggs ended it in the manager's hot-seat following David Moyes' departure. The 40-year-old claimed two wins out of four in his short time in charge and played his final match for United on 6 May 2014 against Hull. He announced his retirement from playing on 19 May, the same day he was named as Louis van Gaal's assistant.

RYAN SIGNS OFF

On 19 May 2014, Giggs penned an open letter to fans as he confirmed his retirement, soon after being named as van Gaal's new no.2...

"Today is a fantastic day for Manchester United. Louis van Gaal is a great appointment and let me begin by telling you how delighted I am to be working with someone of his calibre. His credentials are second to none and I'm positive the club will thrive under his leadership over the coming years.

I would also like to take this opportunity to announce my retirement from professional football and embark upon a new and exciting chapter in my life, as assistant manager of Manchester United. I am immensely proud, honoured and fortunate to have represented the biggest club in the world 963 times and Wales 64 times. My dream was always to play for Manchester United, and although it saddens me to know I won't be pulling on a United jersey again as a player, I have been lucky enough to have fulfilled that dream playing with some of the best players in the world, working under an incredible manager in Sir Alex Ferguson, and most of all, playing for the greatest fans in world football. I have always felt and appreciated your support.

"I want to also give a huge thanks to the backroom staff and support teams we have and have had at Manchester United over the years. I would not have achieved the success I have without your continuing dedication and commitment to creating the best environment to enable the players to thrive. I would not have won 34 trophies in my career without you. I would also like to say a special thanks to my friends and family for all your love and support.

'For me, today is a new chapter filled with mixed emotions - immense pride, sadness, but most of all, excitement towards the future. United fans I hope will share and echo my belief that the club, the management and owners, are doing everything they can to return this great club to where it belongs, and I hope to be there every step of the way. To the greatest fans in world football, thank you, I have loved every minute of playing for you and representing the biggest and best club in the world."

"I can remember vividly when Ryan first broke into the first-team squad - it was clear then that he had the ability to go on and do something very special."
– Bryan Robson

"It was a privilege to have played with him for so many years and now we can turn our thoughts to discussing managerial matters!
– Ole Gunnar Solskjaer

"He's been such a great servant o the game, but more importantly he's been an amazing servant of Manchester United."
– David Beckham

"Ryan is an incredible player and an incredible human being."
– Sir Alex Ferguson

GIGGS – GAMES AND GOALS

	Games	Goals
1990/91	2	1
1991/92	51	7
1992/93	46	11
1993/94	58	17
1994/95	40	4
1995/96	44	12
1996/97	37	5
1997/98	37	9
1998/99	41	10
1999/00	44	7
2000/01	45	7
2001/02	40	9
2002/03	59	14
2003/04	47	8
2004/05	44	8
2005/06	37	5
2006/07	44	6
2007/08	43	4
2008/09	47	4
2009/10	32	7
2010/11	38	4
2011/12	33	4
2012/13	32	5
2013/14	22	0

"For Ryan to have such desire and hunger for success for over 23 years is incredible. He is everything about this club that is great and probably the best player it's ever had."
– Paul Scholes

"Ryan has been a great team-mate, a great friend and a great example for everyone."
– Eric Cantona

"Ryan is an example to all professional players and everyone who plays the game."
– Pele

THE TROPHIES

During his time in the first team, Ryan won…
Champions League – 2
Premier League – 13
FA Cup – 4
League Cup – 3
Intercontinental Cup – 1
Club World Cup – 1
European Super Cup – 1
Charity/Community Shield - 9

FIRST AND LAST…

Games - 2 March 1991 v Everton (H) | 6 May 2014 v Hull City (H)
Goals - 4 May 1991 v Man. City (H) | 23 February 2013 v QPR (A)
Trophies - 19 November 1991 v Red Star Belgrade (N) – European Super Cup
11 August 2013 v Wigan Athletic (N) – Community Shield

ONES TO WATCH

United's ranks are brimming with talented youngsters, and here are five who could be making an impact during the 2014/15 season...

Saidy Janko, Defender

Named the Denzil Haroun Reserve Team Player of the Year in 2013/14, Swiss-born speedster Saidy Janko enjoyed a memorable debut campaign with United. The pacey, athletic youngster joined from FC Zurich in September 2013 after impressing on trial, and quickly displayed his versatility with eye-catching displays in a variety of right-sided positions for the Reds' under-19s and under-21s. "I've settled in pretty well because Manchester United is like a family, so I made friends really quickly," said the defender, for whom hopes are high for an equally impressive second term in England.

Josh Harrop, Midfielder

Stockport-born Josh Harrop is a homegrown United fan whose stock has risen sharply during his time with the Reds' under-18s. His powerful forward bursts from midfield and skill as a provider of chances have long been established, but his game improved most markedly in terms of his goal threat as he grew under Paul McGuinness' tutelage. Nominated for the club's Jimmy Murphy Young Player of the Year award in 2013/14, Harrop is expected to comfortably make the step up to under-21s football, which will provide the perfect platform for his plentiful talent to develop further.

Marcus Rashford, Attacker

Coveted by a host of major clubs but settled with the Reds, attacking midfielder Marcus Rashford is one of the most exciting talents to pass through United's youth system in recent years. Versatile enough to play as a striker or in a slightly withdrawn role, the England youth international made an instant impact when stepping up to FA Youth Cup duty at the age of just 16. A scorer of all manner of goals, Rashford has risen through the United ranks at impressive speed, and his development is expected to continue apace in the 2014/15 season.

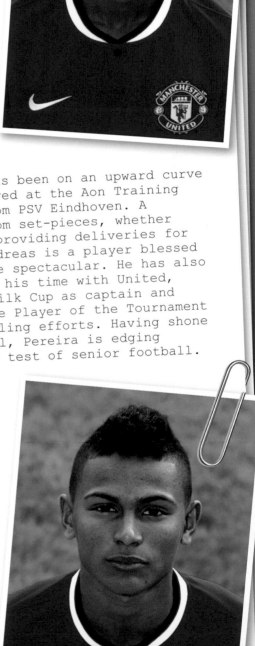

Andreas Pereira, Midfielder

Now in his third season with the Reds, Belgium-born schemer Andreas Pereira's career has been on an upward curve ever since he arrived at the Aon Training Complex in 2012 from PSV Eindhoven. A constant danger from set-pieces, whether going for goal or providing deliveries for his team-mates, Andreas is a player blessed with an eye for the spectacular. He has also sampled success in his time with United, lifting the 2013 Milk Cup as captain and also picking up the Player of the Tournament award for his sterling efforts. Having shone at each youth level, Pereira is edging closer to the acid test of senior football.

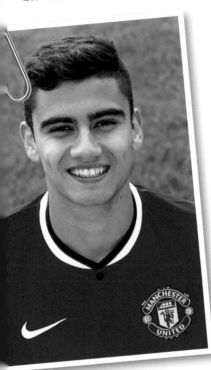

Demetri Mitchell, Winger

An England youth international with pace and skill in abundance, Demetri Mitchell is among the country's hottest young prospects. The Manchester-born left winger has already demonstrated a knack for scoring splendid goals in a variety of ways, but his hallmark is to outstrip defenders with his speed and trickery. Mitchell usually operates on the left flank, but has also been successfully trialled as a centre-forward due to his impressive array of finishing. Now geared up for his second full season in the under-18s, he is expected to kick on in 2014/15 and showcase his talents on a consistent basis.

DEEP IMPACT

Last season, Adnan Januzaj and James Wilson became the latest Academy products to dramatically announce their talents on the senior stage. Here are some of the most eye-catching breakthrough displays from the Reds' homegrown lads in the Premier League era...

PAUL SCHOLES

**21 September 1994,
Port Vale 1 United 2**

One of five teenagers in a controversially much-changed United side for the League Cup trip to Port Vale, 19-year-old Scholes shone as a striker alongside Brian McClair upfront and headlined his debut with a decisive brace. First, the Middleton-born youngster pounced on a short back-pass before clipping in a neat finish to draw the Reds level and then, shortly after half-time, he powered home a match-winning header. Manager Alex Ferguson grinned: "The boy Scholes took his goals superbly," and there would be plenty more such instances as the gifted youngster went on to enjoy one of English football's greatest careers.

DANNY WELBECK

**15 November 2008,
United 5 Stoke City 0**

Danny Welbeck had created a stir throughout his rise through the United ranks, and the clamour to see him blooded in the first team was satisfied by a superb substitute cameo – also his Premier League debut - against Tony Pulis' Potters at Old Trafford. The striker required just half an hour to demonstrate his readiness for the big stage, with the most compelling piece of evidence produced when he picked up the ball midway inside the Stoke half, hurtled forward and thundered an unstoppable 25-yard shot into the Stretford End goal, via the underside of the crossbar. With that, a star was born.

KIKO MACHEDA

**5 April 2009,
United 3 Aston Villa 2**

Though Kiko Macheda departed Old Trafford in the summer of 2014 with just 36 appearances and five goals to show for half a decade in senior football, the impact of his United bow cannot be understated. The Italian striker was a virtual unknown when he entered the fray for an injury-hit United side trailing Aston Villa and struggling to see off the challenge of title rivals Liverpool. Half an hour later, after Cristiano Ronaldo had levelled the scores, 17-year-old Macheda took a place in club folklore with a stunning injury-time winner, curled brilliantly past the flailing Brad Friedel to inject new life into United's title defence.

ADNAN JANUZAJ

5 October 2013,
Sunderland 1 United 2

"Starting Adnan certainly wasn't a gamble for me," said then-United manager David Moyes, after the 18-year-old winger had marked his full Premier League debut with a superb pair of goals to secure three valuable points for the Reds on Wearside. Craig Gardner had opened the scoring and only David De Gea's brilliance had kept the hosts' lead at a single goal, but Januzaj took centre stage after the interval and struck twice in six second-half minutes. His crisp, right-footed equaliser was eye catching, but was nothing in comparison to the fabulous left-footed volley which followed to announce the arrival of a player with limitless potential.

JAMES WILSON

6 May 2014,
United 3 Hull City 1

Interim manager Ryan Giggs – himself a teenage debutant back in 1991 – looked to freshen up his side for the final home game of the 2013/14 campaign, and suggested to his coaching staff that 18-year-old James Wilson could start. "Wilson is unbelievable in the six-yard box," responded coach Nicky Butt, familiar with the striker's prowess from his time working with United's Under-19s. Sure enough, the youngster backed up his coaches' faith, ramming home the opening goal against Steve Bruce's Tigers and tapping in the Reds' second for a close-range brace to mark the start of a career which could just go on to be something very special.

Talk about making an entrance. Just over a decade ago in September 2004, Wayne Rooney announced himself on the Old Trafford stage in quite stunning fashion with a debut hat-trick at the tender age of just 18. The Croxteth-born striker has gone on to rack up over 400 games for the Reds and now sits in the top three of the club's all-time goalscoring list alongside Sir Bobby Charlton and Denis Law with over 200 goals to his name. Here, we take a look back over the club captain's illustrious career to date and hear from the man himself on some of his most famous moments in the red shirt...

DREAM DEBUT

Rooney's United bow was an 'I was there' occasion as the striker netted a memorable hat-trick under the floodlights in the Champions League clash with Turkish outfit Fenerbahce on 28 September 2004. And, as Wayne explains, he was equally delighted with each strike on goal...

Goal 1 – 17 mins

"I remember getting a great pass from Ruud [van Nistelrooy] and it was just instinct to hit it. It was a great feeling to see it end up in the roof of the net."

Goal 2 – 28 mins

"I held back a bit on the edge of the box and received a pass from Giggsy before striking the ball with my right foot into the bottom corner."

Goal 3 - 54 mins

"We got a free-kick about 20 yards out and I just felt like I was going to score. It was a brilliant feeling to curl it in and complete my hat-trick."

GOALS GALORE

1ST GOAL: FENERBAHCE (SEPTEMBER, 2004)

100TH: WIGAN (AUGUST, 2009)

150TH: ARSENAL (AUGUST, 2011)

200TH: BAYER LEVERKUSEN (SEPTEMBER, 2013)

50TH: BOLTON (MARCH, 2007)

Rooney's hit some great strikes over the years, but it's hard to believe anything will ever top his overhead kick which claimed victory in the Manchester derby in February 2011…

"I remember Nani's cross taking a deflection and the ball coming over and just hitting it. You're always working on your technique, but goals like this one are just instinctive. When I was in the air, I remember Berba [Dimitar Berbatov] shouting towards me as if to say 'what are you doing?!' Then I turned round and it was in the top corner. To score a goal like that in a Manchester derby was a great feeling and it's definitely one of the biggest buzzes I've felt after scoring. It has to go down as my favourite goal of my career so far."

MAGIC MOMENTS

Wayne reflects on some stand-out events in his career...

Becoming a Red, 2004

"It took a while to get the deal done, but when I finally signed it felt amazing."

On top of the world, 2008

"Being a world champion at the Club World Cup was a great honour. Scoring the winning goal is something I'm very proud of."

League Cup triumph, 2006

"My first major trophy. We beat Wigan 4-0 in the final and I scored twice - I was over the moon."

THEY SAY...

Rooney's team-mates past and present have spoken glowingly about him over the last decade...

"He's a top performer and a fantastic goalscorer. When I first came to the club, I thought he was a great player, but he's continued to improve again and again and just gets better and better. All credit to him because he's taken on more responsibility over the years and not only does he score goals, he creates them for others as well. He's a great man to have in the team."

– Michael Carrick

"Wayne is a born winner and a player who just loves to score goals. His work-rate for the team is phenomenal and the quality he's got is fantastic. With him in the side you always know you have a chance of scoring a goal and winning a game."

– Darren Fletcher

"You can see the hunger and desire Wayne has to succeed every time he goes out onto the training pitch. That passion is something all the fans love to see from players at this club and Wayne is someone who will give all he can to make sure the team is successful. He loves to score goals but he also gets as much as satisfaction from creating them too if it means the team are doing well. He's someone who always gives 100% to the cause no matter what."

– Ryan Giggs

Moscow memories, 2008

"This was an unbelievable night for the club - I ran straight to Edwin [van der Sar] when he made the save to win us the cup."

Table-toppers, 2011

"I definitely felt a bit of pressure waiting to take this penalty. It gave us a record 19th title and I hope there will be many more to come."

REDS ON TOUR - STATESIDE DIARIES

The players look back on a memorable two-week trip to the US which ended with a trophy...

Louis van Gaal's first task as Manchester United manager was to lead the team across the pond to the United States for a five-game pre-season tour.

After a 7-0 thrashing of LA Galaxy at the famous Rose Bowl Stadium, the Reds came face-to-face with some familiar foes in the International Champions Cup (ICC) tournament. Italian giants AS Roma and Inter Milan were swept aside in Denver and Washington DC respectively, with the clash against Inter providing a reunion with former United captain Nemanja Vidic.

Cristiano Ronaldo and his Real Madrid team-mates also tasted defeat against the Reds in Ann Arbor in front of the biggest crowd ever to watch a football match in the US as over 109,000 fans packed inside the University of Michigan Stadium. A trip to Miami to take on arch rivals Liverpool in the final of the ICC followed two days later as did van Gaal's first piece of silverware as Reds boss as his side came from behind to beat the Merseysiders 3-1 and claim the trophy...

TOUR 2014 PRESENTED BY AON

Results

23 July: **United 7 LA Galaxy 0** (Welbeck, Rooney 2 (1 pen), James 2, Young 2)

26 July: **United 3 AS Roma 2** (Rooney 2 (1 pen), Mata)

29 July: **United 0 Inter Milan 0** (*United win 5-3 on pens)

2 August: **United 3 Real Madrid 1** (Young 2, Chicharito)

4 August: **United 3 Liverpool 1** (Rooney, Mata, Lingard)

LOS ANGELES – JUAN MATA

"I hadn't had a complete pre-season with a team for six or seven years because of summer tournaments so it was nice to do the whole tour of the States.

"Everywhere we go there are always so many fans and we are always so grateful for their support.

"This is the start of a new era for the club. We all enjoy the manager's style of football and hopefully at the end of the season we can celebrate together.

"It was a nice to go to a famous landmark in LA. Our focus in pre-season is always training and matches but it's great to look around the areas we visit as well.

"It was nice to have a visit from an old friend of United's - I call him Sir David Beckham!

"We were all pleased with the result against LA Galaxy but we knew that it was only the first step."

DENVER
– PHIL JONES

"We all enjoyed the training on tour and were keen to impress the boss. We know he wants a passing and moving style and we have a good group of lads willing to learn.

"The tour is a great chance for new players to really settle in and get to know everyone, and that was the case with Ander [Herrera] and Luke [Shaw]. They're both top players and great lads.

"Football is getting bigger in the States all the time and it was nice for the boss to be able to invite some amazing people who do such great work for their cities.

"Facing top-quality teams on tour can only stand you in good stead for the season. All the games were good tests and we were pleased with the hard-fought win against Roma."

WASHINGTON DC – DARREN FLETCHER

"Being on tour was great for me after not having a pre-season for three years. I felt fitter and stronger with every game.

"We're lucky that we get to meet some well-known people in our job and it was a great to catch up with a fellow Scot in DC, tennis player Jamie Murray, Andy's brother.

"The manager expects a lot from us in every training session and every game and thinks we have got the ability to deliver – he believes in us.

"Captaining the side and scoring the winning penalty against Inter was a great feeling. There is a fantastic team spirit amongst everyone and we're all pulling in the right direction."

ANN ARBOR – ASHLEY YOUNG

"As well as training and playing games on tour there are other club commitments and one of mine involved being interviewed by Paddy Crerand for MUTV – we had a good laugh!

"It's always nice to get on the scoresheet and the build-up to the first goal against Real Madrid was fantastic with 20 passes – it was brilliant to finish that off.

"I signed my shirt for the club magazine after the game and made sure Wazza knew that the second goal was mine!

"Playing in front of over 109,000 people was an unbelievable feeling and we were delighted to put on a good performance for them against the European champions."

MIAMI – WAYNE ROONEY

"I was pleased to score in the final and help us win the game. We've had some good results against top opposition so we can be pleased.

"The manager is tough but fair. He has been great since he arrived and has given us all a different way of looking at football.

"It's always nice to beat Liverpool and I was pleased to get the Man of the Match award after the final, but most importantly we were delighted to be coming home with the trophy.

"Everyone worked hard during what was an enjoyable and successful tour which provided us with great preparation for the new season."

WORDSEARCH

There are ten names of United players, past and present, hidden in the grid below, but can you find them?

K M A H K C E B W R
G F G N I L L A M S
V A N P E R S I E P
R P N W X T R M A C
S A N Q B O A R N F
L E F C N T T O O A
L H N A S B K O T T
R J L O E R C N N A
L D M R J L H E A M
O R J B Q H K Y C K

Words go horizontally, vertically, diagonally and backwards.

MATA	JONES	VAN PERSIE	BECKHAM	CANTONA

ROONEY	RONALDO	RAFAEL	STAM	SMALLING

Answers on page 60.

GOING FOR GOAL

Wayne Rooney, Juan Mata and Antonio Valencia are all trying to score, but only one of them can complete the task – can you work out who will find the net?

Answers on page 60.

VAN GAAL QUIZ

How well do you know our manager, Louis van Gaal? Test yourself here...

1. In which year did van Gaal win the Champions League with Ajax?

2. Which former United goalkeeper did he work with during his time with the Dutch side?

3. In what month was van Gaal born?

4. How many times did he win La Liga with Barcelona?

5. He managed the Netherlands at the 2014 World Cup – who did the Dutch beat in their opening match of the tournament?

6. How many other English clubs has van Gaal managed?

Answers on page 61.

SPOT THE BALL

Which do you think is the real ball in this photo?

Answer on page 60.

TRUE OR FALSE?

A: Ryan Giggs scored over 200 goals for United before he retired in May 2014.

B: Old Trafford's North Stand was renamed the Sir Alex Ferguson Stand in 2011.

C: Juan Mata scored United's final goal of the 2013/14 season in a 1-1 draw at Southampton.

D: Phil Jones and Chris Smalling share the same birthday.

E: Wayne Rooney celebrated 10 years as a Red in August 2014.

Answers on page 61.

ANAGRAMS

Unscramble the anagrams to reveal the names of five United legends...

1. Yarn Born Sob

_____

2. Finer Android

_____

3. Bee Egg Sort

_____

4. Wise Land

_____

5. Shark He Mug

_____

Answers on page 61.

SPOT THE DIFFERENCE

Can you work out the six differences between these two photographs?

Answers on page 61.

COMPETITION
WIN A SIGNED SHIRT

Answer the following question correctly and you could be in with the chance of winning a 2014/15 United shirt, signed by some of your favourite players.

QUESTION: How many Premier League titles did United win under Sir Alex Ferguson?

Send your entry and your name on a postcard to the following address or email: muannual2015@manutd.co.uk by midday on 30 April 2015.

2015 Manchester United Annual Signed Shirt Competition
Sir Matt Busby Way Old Trafford
Manchester
M16 0RA

(Please include a daytime telephone number)

The first correct entry picked at random will be the winner. The judge's decision is final. Full terms and conditions apply – please see below.

ANSWERS

WORDSEARCH, PAGE 54

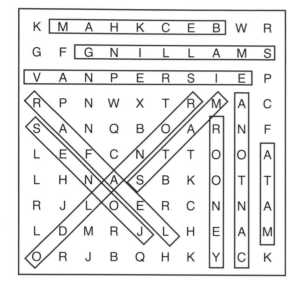

GOING FOR GOAL, PAGE 55

Antonio Valencia scores!

SPOT THE BALL, PAGE 56

VAN GAAL QUIZ, PAGE 56

1. 1995
2. Edwin van der Sar
3. August
4. Twice – 1997/98 and 1998/99
5. Spain
6. None – United are the first English team he has managed.

ANAGRAMS, PAGE 57

1. Bryan Robson
2. Rio Ferdinand
3. George Best
4. Denis Law
5. Mark Hughes

TRUE OR FALSE, PAGE 57

A: False – he ended his career on 168 goals for the Reds.

B: True – it was named after our former manager in November 2011 to mark his 25th anniversary as boss.

C: True – Mata equalised in the 54th minute at St Mary's on 11 May 2014.

D: False – Phil was born on 21 February, while Chris' birthday is on 22 November.

E: True – he signed for United on 31 August 2004.

SPOT THE DIFFERENCE, PAGE 58

FIND FRED

Can you spot Fred the Red in this photo?